SOCCER
SKILLS

FOR AUSSIE KIDS

GARRY POWELL

Wellington

books for kids

Soccer Skills for Aussie Kids

Author: Garry Powell
Illustrator: Darya Kazakova
© 2023 Garry Powell

ISBN: 978 1 925308 91 4 (paperback)
978 1 925308 92 1 (ebook)
Wellington (Aust.) Pty Ltd

ABN 30 062 365 413
433 Wellington Street
Clifton Hill VIC 3068

Love this book?
Visit kidzbookhub.com online to find more great titles.

CONTENTS

HISTORY OF SOCCER

A kicking game like soccer was being played in China thousands of years ago. The game known today as soccer developed in England in the 19th century.

The rules of soccer were established at Cambridge University in 1848, and a group of clubs later formed the Football Association. This type of football spread throughout the world in the 20th century. It became the favourite sport in Europe and South America.

Soccer was first played at the Olympic Games in 1900. Women's soccer became an Olympic sport in the 1996 games in Atlanta.

The first World Championship was played in Uruguay in 1930 and won by the home team.

Soccer is now commonly called the 'World Game' and is the most popular sport in the world.

It became more popular in Australia after World War II when migrants from Europe made 'down under' their new home.

An Association football match.

Team of Sheffield F.C. of 1857. It is the oldest surviving football club in the world.

SOCCER SKILLS

Soccer is a multi-skilled sport.

→ The basic skills are: kicking, trapping, dribbling and heading.
- ◆ kicking
- ◆ trapping
- ◆ dribbling
- ◆ heading

→ Allied skills are: throwing in, goal keeping – stopping, catching, throwing and kicking.
- ◆ throwing in
- ◆ goal keeping – stopping
- ◆ catching
- ◆ throwing
- ◆ kicking

Throwing

Trapping

Kicking

Heading

Dribbling

BASIC SKILLS

Trapping

As the saying goes: 'You have to get the ball before you can use it!'

'Trapping' is receiving and stopping the ball.

The height at which the ball arrives demands how it will be stopped. It can be stopped by all but two parts of the body — arms and hands cannot stop, control or even touch a ball in play.

A low ball is stopped by the inside, outside or bottom of the foot. A bouncing ball is stopped by the legs.

A high ball is trapped using your torso.

→   Watch the ball.

→   Get behind 'the line' of the approaching ball.

→   Decide which part of your body to use to stop the ball.

→   Keep hands and arms wide to help your balance and avoid accidentally touching the ball.

→   Softly cushion the ball as it hits you.

Inside Push Pass

This is passing the ball along the ground to a teammate. It is usually done with a soft push with the foot rather than a kick. A soft push makes it easier for the teammate to control the ball when it arrives.

→ Watch the ball.

→ Contact is made with the middle section of the inside of the foot.

→ Placing the non-kicking foot alongside the ball as it is kicked allows for good balance on the follow through.

→ To keep the ball rolling along the ground, the foot-to-ball contact should be at the central point of the ball.

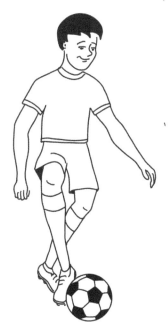

Common faults:

→ Kicking with the toe.

→ Stabbing at the ball instead of pushing it.

→ Kicking from too far behind the ball.

Outside Push Pass

This is a soft short pass.

→ Watch the ball.

→ The ball is pushed by the front half of the outside of the foot.

→ Contact is with the middle of the ball.

→ The pushing action is controlled by the lower leg leading the movement, followed by a flicking of the foot from below the ankle.

→ The ball should be kept in front of the body and to the outside of the passing foot.

Common faults:

→ Not flicking the foot through.

→ Having the ball too far to the side of the body.

→ Contacting too far towards the front or back of the ball and making it spin.

Low Drive

This is to send the ball a greater distance than a short pass. It is a kick rather than a push.

→ Watch the ball.

→ The ball is kicked with the instep holding the ankle stretched and firm.

→ The knee of the kicking leg should be directly above the ball.

→ Contact is made with the middle of the ball.

→ The non-kicking leg takes a long step to land the foot beside the ball.

→ The kicking foot has a long backswing and then a fast forward swing to gain power.

→ The ball is driven forward across the top of the ground.

Common faults:

→ Kicking the bottom of the ball, which makes it go too high.

→ Kicking the side of the ball, which makes it spin and travel in a curved line.

→ Kicking with the toe.

Dribbling

This is pushing the ball along with your feet, keeping it close so that it is always within playing distance (about 1 metre).

→ Watch the ball – after this basic skill is mastered, the ball is moved along without watching it so you can watch your targets.

→ The ball can be pushed with either the inside or outside of the foot.

→ Keep in balance, with weight as evenly spread as possible between both feet.

→ Only move along as fast as you know you can control the ball – walk, jog, run.

HARDER SKILLS

Flick Pass

This is similar to the outside push pass, except with an extra flick on contact with the ball that makes it travel a little faster.

→ Watch the ball into position, glance at the target, then look at the ball again.

→ The ball is flicked by the front half of the outside of the foot.

→ Contact is with the middle of the ball.

→ The ball should be kept in front and outside of the flicking foot.

Common faults:

→ Flicking the ball (the ankle needs to be kept stiff).

→ Having the ball too far to the front or the side.

→ Contacting the side of the ball, which can make it spin and travel in a curved path.

Lofted Drive

This is used to send the ball a longer distance either to a teammate or just to gain territory.

→   Watch the ball.

→   The ball is kicked with the instep, with the ankle stretched and firm.

→   Approach the ball slightly from the side.

→   Contact the bottom half of the ball.

→   The kicking foot has a long backswing and a fast follow through to gain power.

→   The knee straightens on impact with the ball.

→   Leg follows through towards the target.

Volley

This is kicking the ball that arrives before it bounces – on the full.

→   Watch the ball.

→   Contact is made with the instep for long volleys and the inside of the foot for shorter kicks.

→   The body is either behind the line of flight of the ball or a little to the side.

→   The ball is kept low by bending the leg after contact.

→   Contact the middle or top half of the ball.

→   When kicking from the side, the body leans slightly backward.

→ The leading shoulder should point to the target as contact is made.

→ For longer kicks, the follow-through should be longer.

Half Volley

This is one of the more difficult kicking skills, as it is done from a high ball.

→ Watch the ball.

→ Time the kick to be exactly as the ball lands.

→ The approach of the kicker is the hardest part – to reach the landing spot before the ball.

→ Contact can be with the outside, inside or instep of the foot – depending on the direction of the kick needed.

→ The non-kicking foot should be alongside the ball on contact.

Chip Pass

This is another difficult skill. It is a pass that is lobbed gently to a teammate.

→ Watch the ball.

→ Kick with the instep, with a bent and relaxed ankle and knee of the kicking foot.

→ Approach the ball from behind or slightly to the side.

→ The non-kicking foot should be alongside the ball as contact is made with the kicking foot.

→ If it is a long pass, there is a long follow-through with the kicking leg.

→ Contact must be made under the ball to make it slightly backspin and rise steeply.

Shoot

This is a fast and powerful kick at the goal.

→ Watch the ball.

→ There are four types of shots: low drive, high drive, hard (powerful) volley, swerve ball.

→ A drive is a kick that makes the ball travel fast. A low drive aims at the inside bottom corners of the net and the high drive at the inside top corners.

→ A hard volley is used to surprise a goalkeeper who might be expecting a drive after the ball has bounced.

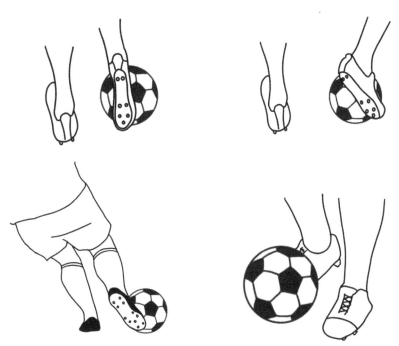

→ A swerve ball travels in a curved flight path, and is used to confuse a goalkeeper as to its travel. It is kicked by contacting one side of the ball.

- Contact by the outside of the right foot will make the ball curve from left to right.
- Contact by the inside of the right foot will make the ball curve from right to left.

Header

This is striking the ball with the head. It is a skill seldom used in junior soccer because of potential injury.

→ To learn, a soft and light ball should be used: nerf ball, volleyball, playball or beachball.

→ Older teens sometimes learn using a soccer ball with some air let out to make it softer. A proper soccer ball should only be used when the skill level is good.

→ Watch the ball.

→ Contact should be made with the forehead.

→ The neck is kept firm and the head nods through the ball.

→ Power can be made by flexing and straightening the knees on contact.

The Throw

A throw is used to bring the ball back into play after it has gone out of bounds over the sidelines. It is taken by a team member of the opposite team that had last touch of the ball before it went out.

A goalkeeper can also throw the ball to a teammate after taking possession inside the goal 'penalty area'.

→ From the sidelines a throw must be made with two hands (double) from behind the head.

→ Feet must remain on the ground.

- → A goalkeeper may throw or roll the ball with double or single hands.

- → A throw along the ground makes it easier for a teammate to control the ball.

- → A high throw is to gain distance.

Goalkeeper

Player from sideline

SKILL PRACTICE FOR ONE PLAYER

Trap

These exercises help with the control of an incoming ball.

→ Ball sit – sitting on the ball helps to get a 'feel' of the ball itself.

→ Ball juggling – while staying more or less in the same spot, bounce the ball from:

- Foot to foot
- Knee to knee
- Foot to knee
- Right foot to left knee
- Left foot to right knee
- Right foot to right knee
- Left foot to left knee
- Foot to head
- Knee to head
- Foot – knee – head
- Continuous juggling – how many passes of each kind can be done in a row

→ Ball awareness:

- Roll the ball, chase after it and stop it with one foot.
- Throw the ball against a wall and trap the return.
- Kick the ball against a wall and trap the return.
- Kick the ball and trap it – after two bounces, one bounce, on the full.
- Drop the ball then kick it up to catch it – vary the height of the bounce before the kick, and vary the height the kick goes.
- Pull the ball towards you using one foot and flick it up to catch it. Use the right foot then the left.

Dribble

These exercises help with moving along with the ball.

→ Dribble the ball while walking slowly. Stop the ball with one foot after 10 touches.

→ Dribble while jogging.

→ Dribble and try to keep the ball just in your side vision.

→ Dribble while running.

→ Dribble:
  - Right foot only
  - Left foot only
  - Alternate feet: left–right, left–right.
  - Insides of the feet only
  - Outsides of the feet only
  - Mixed insides and outsides of the feet

→ Dribble around an obstacle course.

→ Dribble along a line.

→ Dribble on the lines completely around a court or soccer pitch.

Pass

The best friend a player can have when practising by themselves is a wall or hard fence that will rebound a ball.

By passing or kicking the ball against such an obstacle, the ball rebounds without having to be 'fetched'.

→ Inside foot pass:
  - Pass a stationary ball at a wall.
  - Pass a slowly moving ball.
  - Pass between two blocks.
  - Pass at a target on the wall.

Wall

- Change the distance from the wall.
- Change the angle to the target.
- Pass a bouncing ball.
- Use right foot only, left foot only, alternate feet.

→ Outside foot pass:

- The same activities done for an inside foot pass are done for an outside foot pass.

Kicking and Shooting

→ Against a friendly rebound wall:

- Kick a stationary ball
- Kick a slowly moving ball
- Use left foot, right foot, alternate feet.

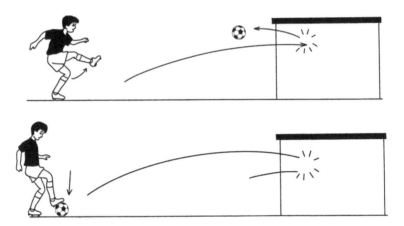

→ Kick at a target.

→ Vary the distance and height of the target.

→ Vary the power of the kick or drive.

→ Trap the rebound and repeat.

→ Kick/shoot very hard.

→ Kick with a swerve shot.

→ Return kick a rebound without first trapping the ball.

→ How many in a row?

→ Volley against the wall.

→ Half volley against the wall.

Heading

Always use a soft ball – nerf ball, volleyball, beach ball.

→ Throw the ball into the air – head it up again and catch it.

→ Throw into the air – head it up and head again.

→ Juggle the ball using headers.

→ Juggle from foot to head.

→ Bounce the ball hard and then head it.

→ Throw gently high against the wall and head the return.

→ Head at a target – low, high, angled.

Throw

As for kicking – use a wall to rebound the ball.

→ Double-hand throw against the wall. Vary the power
  • Vary the distance
  • Vary the height
  • Vary the angle

→ Throw at a target.

→ Throw and catch the rebound.

→ Throw to bounce the ball before the wall.

→ Practise goalkeeper one-hand throws.

Stop – Trap

These are all done from rebounds against a wall.

→ Roll a ball against the wall and trap the rebound:
- ◆ With one foot (any foot)
- ◆ Right foot only
- ◆ Left foot only
- ◆ Sole of the foot
- ◆ Both feet together to form a wedge.

→ Underarm throw against the wall and trap the rebound:

- With one foot
- With one leg
- Both legs
- After the ball bounces two or three times
- After one bounce
- On the full (before it bounces)
- Vary the throws by distance, power and height.

→ Overhead double-hand throws against the wall and trap the rebound

- All the variations as for the underarm throws.

→ Kick against the wall and trap the rebound:

- All the variations as for the throws.
- Repeats – develop a pattern – trap, then kick again.

SKILL PRACTICE WITH A PARTNER

Stop – Trap

Using one ball between the two players. Take it in turns to be the thrower/kicker and trapper.

→ Trap a ball rolled by a partner:
- ◆ One foot, both feet
- ◆ Having to move (run) to get to the ball

→ Stop a ball thrown by a partner:
- ◆ Underarm throw
- ◆ Double-hand overhead throw
- ◆ After two or three bounces, one bounce, on the full.

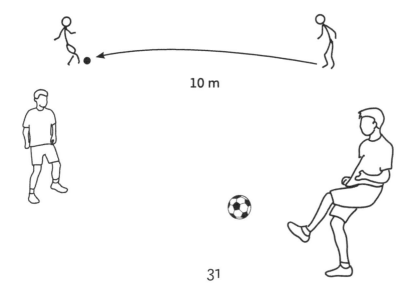

10 m

→ Stop a ball kicked by a partner:

- ◆ Change the distance, speed and angle of the incoming ball.

→ Develop a pattern: stop – kick – stop – kick:

→ How many can be done in a row?

- ◆ On the move: staying about 10 metres apart, partners move the length of a court or pitch stopping and passing the ball to each other with the inside of their foot as they go – walking, jogging.
- ◆ Then by returning to the other end of the area, again passing and stopping as they go means partners use the other foot.

Pass

A pass should be fast enough to get to the partner, but not so fast that it is hard to control.

All these practices should be done with the four types of pass: inside and outside foot passes and left and right foot.

The passing distance should at first be about 2–3 metres.

→ Pass to a partner who is stationary.

→ Pass over a marker.

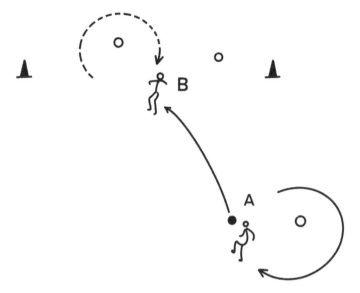

→ Pass to a partner who is moving – this means to aim a little ahead.

→ Pass with a stationary ball, a moving ball, a bouncing ball.

→ Pass while you are moving and the partner is still. Pass while you are both moving.

→ Reduce the distance to 1–2 metres.

→ Increase the distance to 8–10 metres.

→ Continuous passing between moving partners.

→ Control the ball with one foot and pass back with the other.

→ Pass between partners without trapping the ball first.

→ Pass and move – this exercise is to help players look for each other, and time their runs to the ball. Played on an area about 10 × 10 metres, with two markers on each of the four sides of the pitch.

- The first player dribbles the ball around one of these side markers.
- The other player runs around a marker on a different side of the pitch and then into the playing area.
- The first player on re-entering the pitch passes to their partner, who has also re-entered the playing area.
- The players then swap roles, but dribble and run around different side markers.

Kick

As with all practice skills – both sides of the body should be used equally. The following should be varied:

Short kick – long kick

Slow kick – fast kick

Low kick – high kick

Curved ball – left and right.

→ Kick a stationary ball.

→ Kick a moving ball.

→ Kick to a partner who is standing still.

→ Kick to a moving partner.

→ Return kick – kick – stop the ball – return kick – each
partner in sequence.

→ Kick while both moving to make a zig-zag pattern.

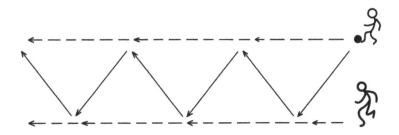

Shoot

This is a favourite skill to practise, as everyone likes to score a goal. The kick used is normally a hard and fast kick.

In practice there should always be a 'backstop' (wall, fence or net) to save having to fetch balls.

The goal dimensions are: 7.32 × 2.44 metres.

→ Even though shots will be mostly hard and fast kicks, many types should be practised:

• Left and right foot

• Fast and slow

- ◆ High and low into the corners
- ◆ From short and long distances
- ◆ Left and right curving balls.

→ If no actual soccer goal is available:
- ◆ A goal can be marked on a wall
- ◆ Markers can be put down in front of a fence.

→ One partner shoots and the other acts as a goalkeeper and tries to stop the ball.

Dribbling

→ Follow the leader:

- Using only one ball – take it in turns to do the same trick.

- With a ball each – one partner follows behind the other copying exactly the movements and skills of the first player.

- Side by side – copying the leader not from behind but beside.

- Take turns as leader.

→ Dribble races – set a course and dribble around it:

- Along a line

- Around an obstacle such as a marker, goal or shed

- Through a set obstacle course

- A zig-zag course.

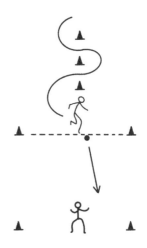

→ Dribble and shoot – each partner tries to score in a proper sized goal.

- This practice or race can be done with either both players dribbling at the same time or by timing each player over the same course.

→ One on one – in a set space such as a third of a court or pitch.

- ♦ The player without the ball tries to win the ball from the other and then shoot a goal. No body contact is allowed.

Heading

All heading practices should be done with a light, soft ball – nerf ball, volleyball, beach ball – until the skills are very good.

→ One partner tosses the ball to themselves and then heads it to their partner.

→ Head a ball that is gently thrown by a partner.

→ Head a ball while both partners are walking.

→ Head to each other:
- ♦ On the spot
- ♦ While walking.

→ 10 up – try for 10 headers in a row.

GROUP PRACTICE AND GAMES

Attack and Defend

→   2 on 2 (4 players)

- Played on an area about the size of a basketball court or half of a soccer pitch.
- This game uses a combination of dribbling, passing and shooting.

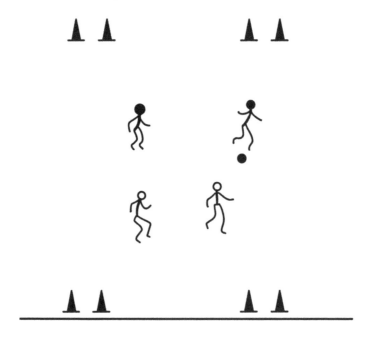

- There are two goals at each end. Each pair has an attacking end and a defending end.
- One pair starts with the ball at the middle side of the court. They attack – **the other pair defends**. A goal can be scored through either of the goal markers at their attacking end.
- After two minutes the pairs swap roles from attackers to defenders.

→ 3 on 3 (6 players)
- One goal at each end and one of each trio is a goalkeeper.

Five Trips (3 players)

To practise passing and trapping.

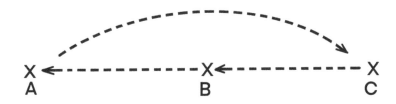

→ Player C passes the ball to player B. Player B traps the ball, turns and passes it to player A.
- Player A traps the ball and returns it to player B.

Player B traps the ball again, turns and passes it back to player C. This is one trip.

• After five trips players change starting positions.

→ One variation can be player C to player B, to player A. Then player A all the way back to player C, and so on.

Corner Spry (4–6 players)

To practise passing and trapping.

→ The leader passes the ball to each player in turn. They trap the ball and return pass back to the leader.

→ When number 5 gets the ball, they don't return it – they dribble the ball out to the front of the group to become the new leader.

→ All players move down one place as no. 5 leaves (the old leader goes to no. 1, no. 1 to no. 2, 2 to 3, 3 to 4, 4 to 5).

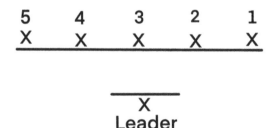

Rebound Ball (4–8 players)

Kicking and trapping.

→   Player 1 kicks the ball against the wall and moves to the end of the line.

→   Payer 2 traps the rebound ball and in turn kicks it back against the wall.

→   Then player 3 and so on.

Shuttle Kick (4–8 players)

Passing, kicking, trapping and dribbling.

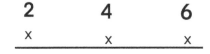

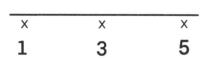

→   Player 1 kicks the ball to player 2 and follows across to take no. 2's place.

→ No. 2 kicks the ball to no. 3 and runs over to take no. 3's place and so on.

→ When no. 8 or the last player receives the ball, they dribble the ball around to the empty no. 1 spot, and the cross-shuttle begins again.

→ This series continues until all players are back in their original position.

Soccer Skittles (4–8 players)

To practise kicking and shooting.

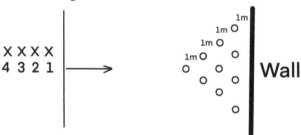

Starting line

```
X X X X
4 3 2 1
```

Wall

→ Ten cones or blocks are placed 1 metre ahead and to the side of each other in a 'V' formation.

→ Marks should be placed underneath the cones so they can quickly be replaced.

→ Singles – one at a time, each player has one kick to see how many skittles they can knock down.

→ Chances – each player continues to kick until all the cones are down.

→ The distance between the kicker and the targets can increase as the skills improve.

Circle Dribble (6–16 players)

Dribble and player awareness practice.

→ A circle about 20 metres across is marked out. Players line up just inside the edge of the circle. Every second player has a ball.

→ Each player dribbles their ball across the circle to lay off (pass) to a player without the ball. This player takes possession and dribbles across to a different player who now doesn't have a ball.

→ All players need to be aware of other players in the circle, as several will be crossing at the same time.

Dribble Relays (8–24 players)

To encourage speed and control of the ball.

→ The relay course can be between lines, around a court, across a pitch or around obstacles.

→ Before an actual relay race, all players should have a few turns without time involved.

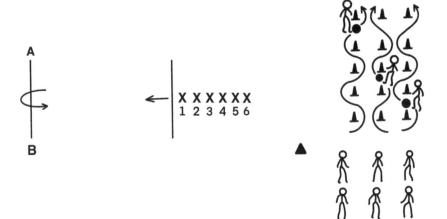

Squares (12–18 players)

Dribble and awareness practice.

→ A square is marked out – about 10 × 10 metres. Each player has a ball.

→ On command, all players dribble their ball across

the square to the other side and then back to their starting position.

→ This can create great mix-ups – it is not a race. A successful cross without losing control of the ball is the aim.

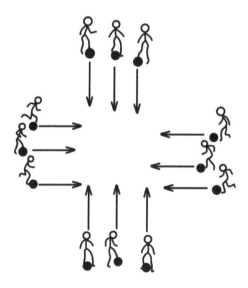

Captain Dodge Ball (12–18 players)

To practise throw ins and intercepts.

→ The group is divided into two teams. There is one ball.

→ The throwing team is evenly spaced around the outside of a 20-metre circle. The defending team

are scattered inside the circle. The leader of the defending team stands on a spot in the centre of the circle.

→ The throwing team throw or roll the ball to try to hit the leader below the waist.

→ The defending team protect their leader by foot or leg.

→ If the leader is hit, they remain on the spot, but two defenders are put out of the circle.

→ If a defender is hit above the waist they are also out and must leave the circle. After a minute the defenders are counted – one defender equals one point.

→ Teams change roles.

→ Variations:

  • A target instead of a leader
    Use 2–3 balls.

Corner Kick Ball (12–18 players)

This game is ideally played on a netball court which has equal thirds. Otherwise, divide a basketball court or third of a soccer pitch into three equal sections.

→ A ball is placed in the centre of the middle section. The two teams stand on their baseline/goal line.

→ On command, the two end players (one from each end) of both teams run into the middle section and try to kick the ball over their opponent's goal line.

→ These four players must stay in the middle section. The other players try to stop the ball going over their goal line from within their own end sections. When in the end sections, players can use their body or hands to stop the ball. They then try to pass it to one of their centre teammates.

- a player crosses their team's dividing line
- the ball is kicked higher than shoulder height.

→ Rough play.

- After a goal is scored, the ball is returned to the centre – the old centre players retire to the middle of their lines – two new end players from each team race to the centre on command. They become the four new centre players.

Kick Tag (8–18 players)

This game is played on a basketball court or a third of a soccer pitch.

→ Four balls are used and should be softer than a regular soccer ball – volleyballs or beachballs are suggested.

→ Four players are selected as attackers. Their task is to tag the other players below the knees with the ball. The game can be played with one ball between attackers, or with each of the four attackers having a ball.

→ Any player tagged then becomes a tagger as well, and balls can be passed between taggers.

→ Attackers can either dribble or kick their ball.

→ The last player tagged is the new leader and they choose three other players to be the new attackers (any one person can only be an attacker once).

→ If an attacker touches a ball with their hands, the last person tagged goes free. Free players are not allowed outside the playing area.

Passers versus Dribblers (12–18 players)

The group is split into two teams – one team to be dribblers and the other passers.

→   The dribbling team is in a line, and the passing team are in a circle around a leader. On the command START, the first dribbler runs around the circle while controlling the ball with their feet. Each member of the dribbling team does the same in turn.

→   When all dribblers have been around the circle, their leader (first dribbler) yells STOP.

→ The passing team has been counting the passes between their leader and outside players.

→ Teams then change places. The team with the greater number of passes is the winner.

→ For the next game change the leaders.

→ The game can be varied by changing the size of the circle for the passing team, or limiting passing to left or right foot only.

Dribbling Rounders (8–12 players)

This game is best on an area the size of a basketball court or a third of a soccer pitch. Markers are used to show the dribble paths for both teams.

→ Two balls are used.

→ Players are divided into batting (kicking) and fielding (controlling) teams. The kicking team is in a line, with one player in the 'batting box'. The returning team is spread throughout the playing area with one member in the 'goal box'.

→ Number 1 batter kicks one ball into the field of play, then immediately dribbles the second ball around the outside markers.

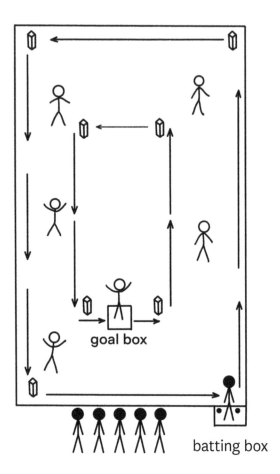

goal box

batting box

→ The fielding team must stop the first ball and pass it to their number 1 fielder, who is in the goal box. As soon as number 1 fielder receives the ball inside the box, they dribble this ball around the inside markers. Each circuit of the inside markers scores a point.

→ Number 1 fielder stops his dribbling when the number 1 batter is back in their box and yells STOP.

→ Then the number 2s take over, and so on. Teams swap roles after once through the batters.

Rules:

→ The first kick cannot go outside the field of play.

→ No player may handle the ball.

→ The batter cannot be obstructed.

  • If a marker is knocked over, it must be replaced by the dribbler before they can continue.

Change Soccer (6–12 players)

This game is played in a small area such as a volleyball court or half a basketball court.

→ Each team is divided into numbered pairs (1, 2, 3, 4) and sits behind its goal. The ball is on a spot in the middle of the playing area.

→ On command GO, the first pair of each team runs to the middle and try to score a goal at their opponents' end.

→ Both teammates must touch the ball before they can shoot for goal.

→ Soccer rules apply.

→ When a goal is scored, the ball is replaced on the centre spot and the next pair await the GO command.

→ A variation can be played with the referee calling another number while the first pair are still playing. This means there will be four players from each team in the playing area instead of just two.

Circle Soccer (10–18 players)

Two equal teams.

→ Best played in a gym or a fenced area so that balls don't have to be fetched. A special playing area needs to be marked out:

→ A circle of 8 metres diameter inside a second circle of 10 metres diameter, with a centre line across both.

→ Teams line up on opposite sides of the centre line and between the two circles. This between the two circles is the 'kicking' area.

→ On command, the ball is rolled into the centre of one of the kicking areas. That team tries to score a goal by kicking it through their opponents' area below shoulder height.

→ Soccer rules apply.

→ Players must remain in their own kicking area and are not permitted into the inner circle.

Scoring:

→ Each goal is a point.

→ Opponents score a point if a player steps inside the centre circle, kicks the ball above shoulder height, or touches the ball with hands or arms.

Try Scores (6–12 players)

Played on a basketball court or a third of a soccer pitch.

→ Two even teams.

→ This game is played 3 versus 3 on a volleyball court or 6 versus 6 on a basketball court.

→ Soccer rules apply.

→ The game starts at one end of the court, with one team attacking and the other defending. The defending team cannot score a goal.

→ After one minute or when a try is scored, teams change roles.

→ Players score a try by passing the ball around to be trapped by one of their teammates who is over the goal line.

Four Goal Soccer (6–12 players)

Played on a basketball court or a third of a soccer pitch.

→ There is one goal on each of the four sides of the playing area and a goalkeeper for each.

→ Each team attacks two adjacent goals and defends the other two. The goalkeeper starts play again after a goal is scored.

→ Teams take turns in starting with the ball. Soccer rules apply (still no offside rule).

Attackers versus Defenders – Quarters (9–12 players)

Played on a basketball court or a third of a soccer pitch. Divide the playing area into four equal parts (quarters).

→ Six attackers versus three defenders. These defenders must wear vests or colour bands to show their team colours.

→ Four of the attackers (numbers 1, 2, 3, 4) are restricted to only one quarter of the court (their home). Two attackers (numbers 5, 6) are 'free rein' and can go anywhere.

→ The three defenders are also 'free rein' and can go into any of the four quarters.

→ The attackers pass the ball between teammates while the defenders try to gain possession from them.

→   Scoring is the number of successful passes made by the attackers.

→   When possession is lost or after a one-minute time period, three of the attackers swap with three of the defenders, and so on.

Attackers versus Defenders – Halves (9–12 players)

Played on a basketball court or a third of a soccer pitch. Divide the playing area into halves.

→   There are six attackers and three defenders. Of the attackers, two must remain in each of their home halves (1, 2) in one half and (3, 4) in the other. Two attackers (5, 6) are 'free rein' and can go into either half to follow the ball. All defenders are 'free rein'.

→   Scoring is the number of successful passes made by the attackers.

→   When possession is lost or after a two-minute time period, three attackers swap with three defenders, and so on.

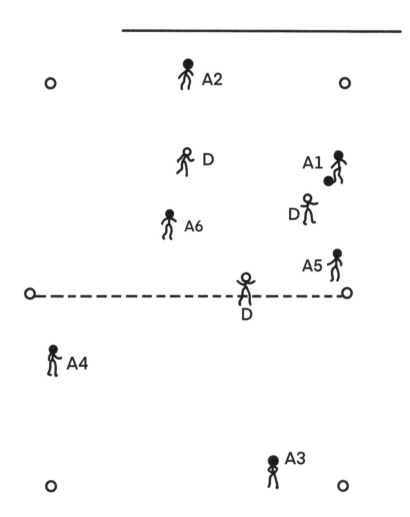

Mini Soccer (6–12 players)

This game is played on half of a soccer pitch.

→ This is a game where most of the official rules of soccer can be introduced. It can be played 3 on 3, 4 on 4, 5 on 5, or 6 on 6. Each team has a goalkeeper, and defence and forward players.

→ It can be played: many touch, 3 touch, 2 touch or 1 touch (the number of touches a player can have before passing to a teammate).

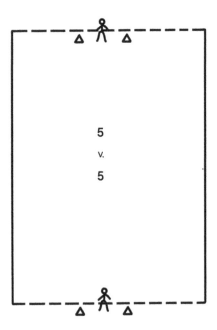

SOCCER: THE WORLD GAME

Played by two teams of 11 players – 10 field players and one goalkeeper each. An adult soccer pitch/ground can vary in a range between 60 × 100 yards (45 × 90 metres) and 100 × 130 yards (90 × 120 metres). The maximum size for youth soccer is 55 × 100 yards (20 × 90 metres), and the minimum size is 15 × 30 yards (14 × 23 metres).

→ The size of the soccer pitch varies with the age of the players.

Age	Field size (yards)	Ball size
Adult	60 × 100	5
U-14	55 × 80	5
U-12	50 × 80	4
U-10	40 × 70	4
U-8	25 × 50	3
U-6	15 × 30	3

→ The aim of the game is to get the ball into the opponents' goal (the goal the opponents are defending).

→ The 10 field players are not allowed to touch the ball with their hands or arms while it is in play. The goalkeeper alone can use their upper limbs when the ball is inside the penalty area.

→ There are 17 basic rules. (Look up 'laws of the game' reference.)

→ The tricky rule that is brought in for teenager and adult soccer is the offside rule: offside is called when an attacking player is in front of the last defender when a teammate passes to them when inside the opponent's half.

→ A field player cannot be called offside in their own half of the pitch. The goalkeeper does not count as a defender.

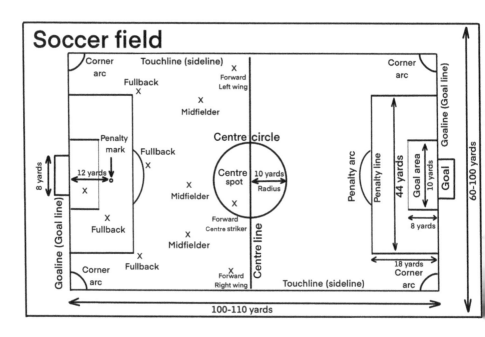

Eat to Play

→ Eat regular meals.

→ Eat lots of different foods from different food types.

→ Eat for energy – the more you exercise, the more fuel your body needs.

→ Eat only small amounts of fatty and sugary foods.

→ Eat lots of fresh fruits, grains and vegetables.

→ Drink lots of water.

WARM UP AND WARM DOWN

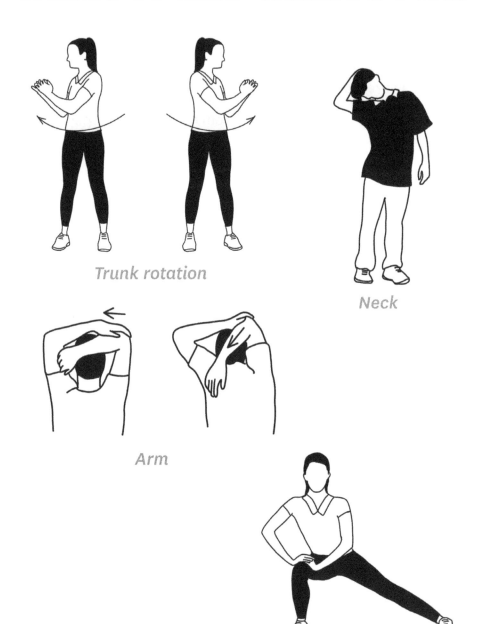

Trunk rotation

Neck

Arm

Inner thigh

Thigh

Calf

Hamstring

Lower back

SOCCER TALK

attacker – a player on the team that has the ball

backs – players who defend

ball – for adults: about 69 centimetres in circumference and 430 grams in weight

centre spot – where the kick-off is taken

corner kick – a direct free kick taken by an attacker when a defender or the goalkeeper is the last to touch the ball over the end line

cross – a pass from the side of the pitch to an attacker to shoot at goal

defender – a player on the team that has not got possession of the ball

dress – team uniform

dribble – moving and keeping the ball close to the feet

drive – a hard, fast kick

forward – a player who attacks

foul – an indirect free kick, usually due to a player's contact with another

free kick – penalty from a foul

goal – when the ball passes over the goal line

goalkeeper (goalie) – the one member of the team who plays mainly in the penalty area and can touch a ball in play with their upper limbs

goal kick – taken by a defender when an attacker is the last player to touch the ball over the end line

goal lines – the end lines between the goal posts

half volley – kicking a bouncing ball just as it touches the ground

hand ball – a free kick when a field player handles a ball 'in play'

header – hitting the ball with the head

kick – contacting the ball with either foot

offside – in adult soccer when an attacking player does not have two of their opponents between themselves and the goal

pass – to kick a ball to a teammate

pitch – the ground where a soccer field is marked out

referee – the umpire in charge of the game

shoot – a kick at goal

throw-in – to restart play from the sideline

trap – to stop and control the ball

volley – kicking a ball while it is in the air

warm up – exercises to get the body warm before play

warm down – exercises to help cool the body down after play

Printed in Australia
Ingram Content Group Australia Pty Ltd
AUHW020950281223
388345AU00001B/3

9 781925 308914